The Best of Belwin Jazz

JAZZ BAND SERIES COLLECTION

1st E♭ Alto Saxophone

Contents

*Page numbers in each book vary;
therefore, each player must refer to the contents page in his or her own book.*

Get It On	12
Greensleeves	26
Jumpin' At The Woodside	20
Just In Time	8
Lester Leaps In	2
My Foolish Heart	10
Oh, Lady Be Good!	16
On Green Dolphin Street	6
Summertime	24
This Can't Be Love	14

Alfred Music Publishing Co., Inc.
16320 Roscoe Blvd., Suite 100
P.O. Box 10003
Van Nuys, CA 91410-0003
alfred.com

© 2009 BELWIN-MILLS PUBLISHING CORP.,
a division of ALFRED MUSIC PUBLISHING CO., INC.
All Rights Reserved Including Public Performance

ISBN-10: 0-7390-6663-3
ISBN-13: 978-0-7390-6663-8

Any duplication, adaptation or arrangement of the compositions contained in this book requires the written consent of the Publisher.
No part of this book may be photocopied or reproduced in any way without permission.
Unauthorized uses are an infringement of the U.S. Copyright Act and are punishable by law.

LESTER LEAPS IN

1ST Eb ALTO SAXOPHONE

By LESTER YOUNG
Arranged by RICH SIGLER

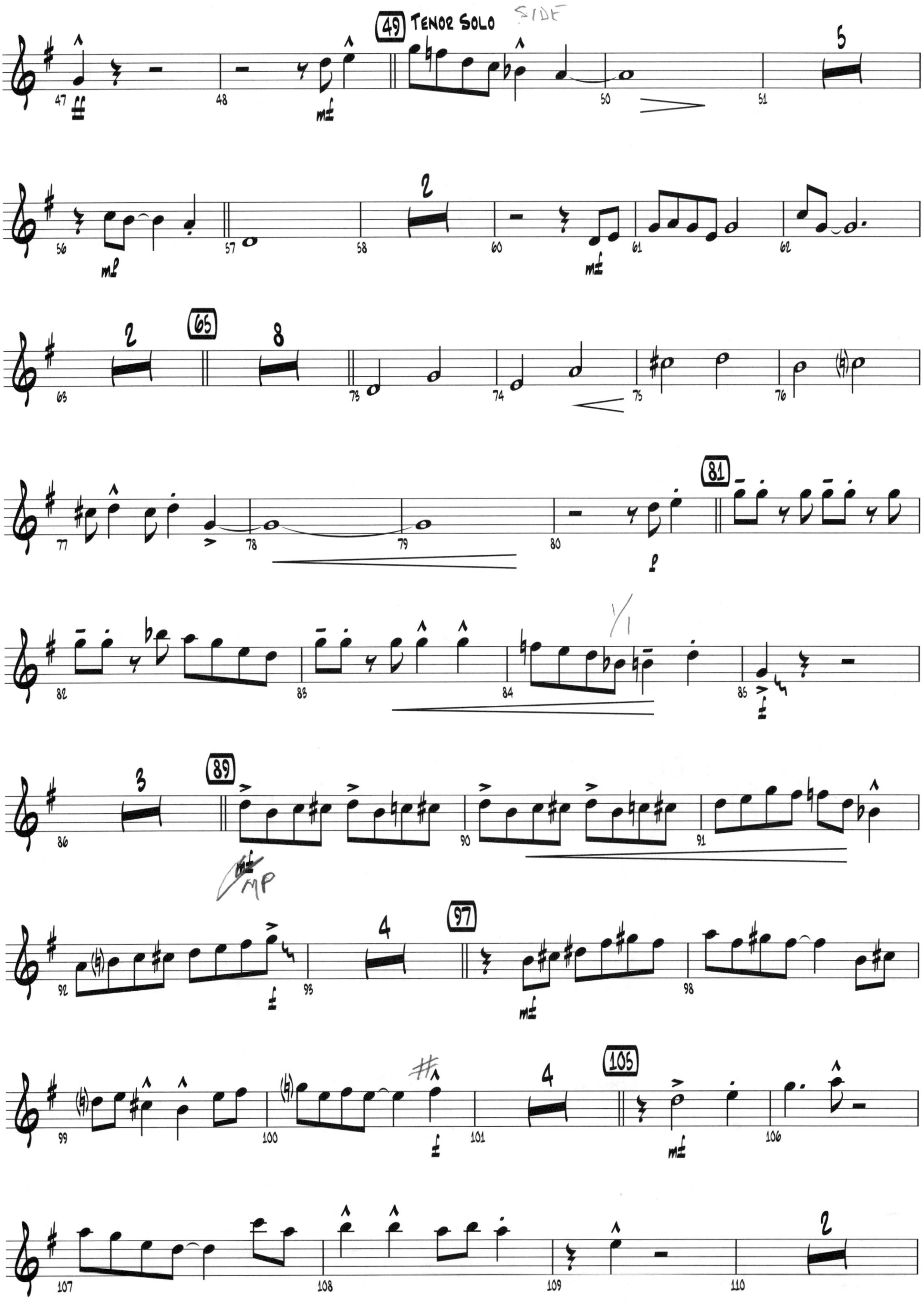
49
TENOR SOLO
65
81
89
97
105

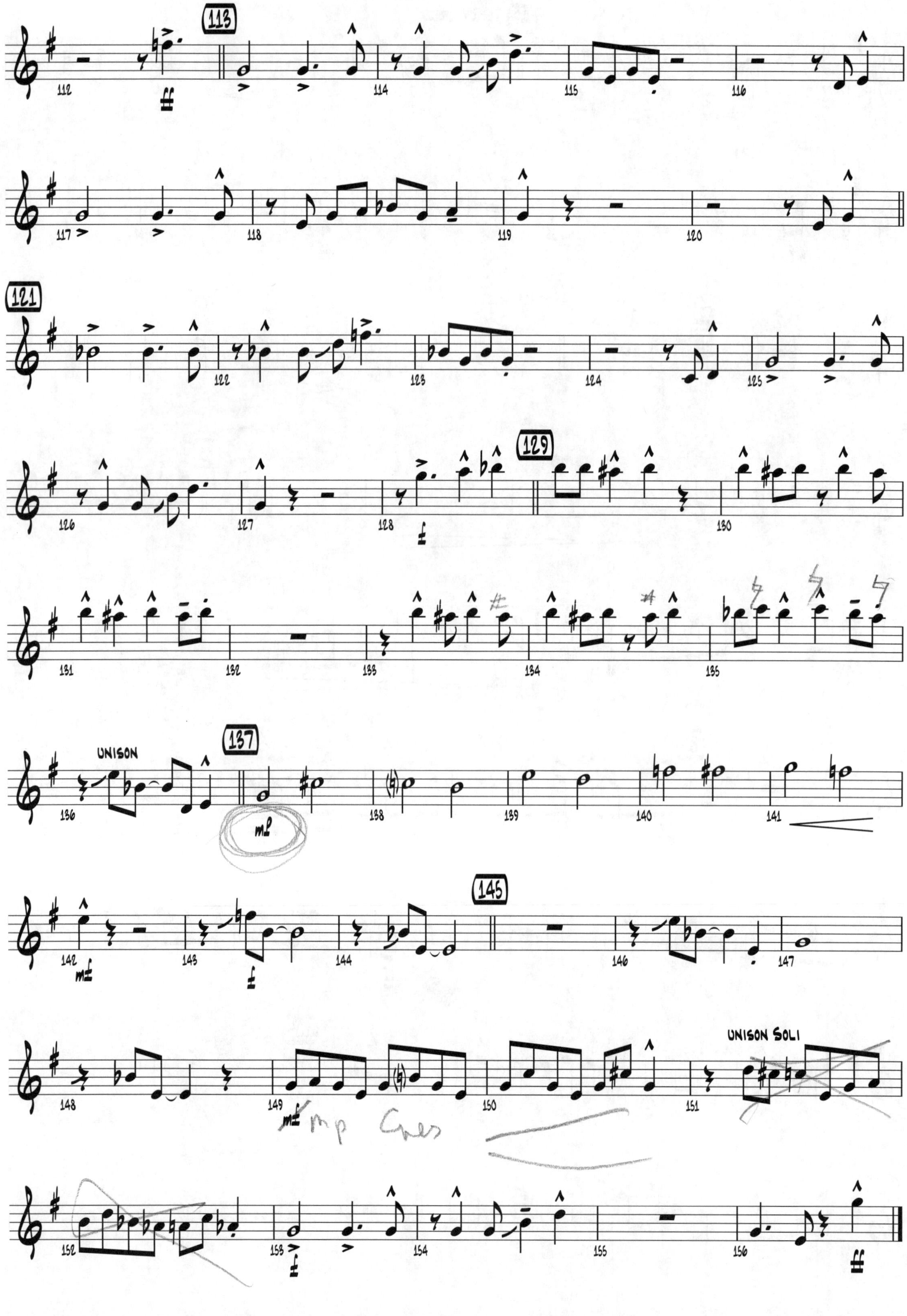
113
121
129
UNISON
137
145
UNISON SOLI
mp
Cues

This page left blank intentionally to facilitate page turns.

ON GREEN DOLPHIN STREET

1st Eb Alto Saxophone

Music by BRONISLAU KAPER
Lyrics by NED WASHINGTON
Arranged by DAVE WOLPE

© 1947 (Renewed) METRO-GOLDWYN-MAYER INC.
All Rights Controlled by EMI FEIST CATALOG INC. (Publishing)
and ALFRED MUSIC PUBLISHING CO., INC. (Print)
This arrangement © 2008 EMI FEIST CATALOG INC.
and ALFRED MUSIC PUBLISHING CO., INC.
All rights Reserved Including Public Performance

CMAJ9
EMI7
A7(b9)
1.
2.
DMI7
DMI7/C
BMI7(b5)
E7(b9)
AMI7
AMI7/G
F#MI7(b5)
B7(b9)
EMI7
A7
DMI7
G7
C
59
SOLI
1.
SOLI
2.
UNIS.
SOLI
UNIS.

JUST IN TIME

1st E♭ Alto Saxophone

Lyrics by BETTY COMDEN and ADOLPH GREEN
Music by JULE STYNE
Arranged by W. SCOTT RAGSDALE

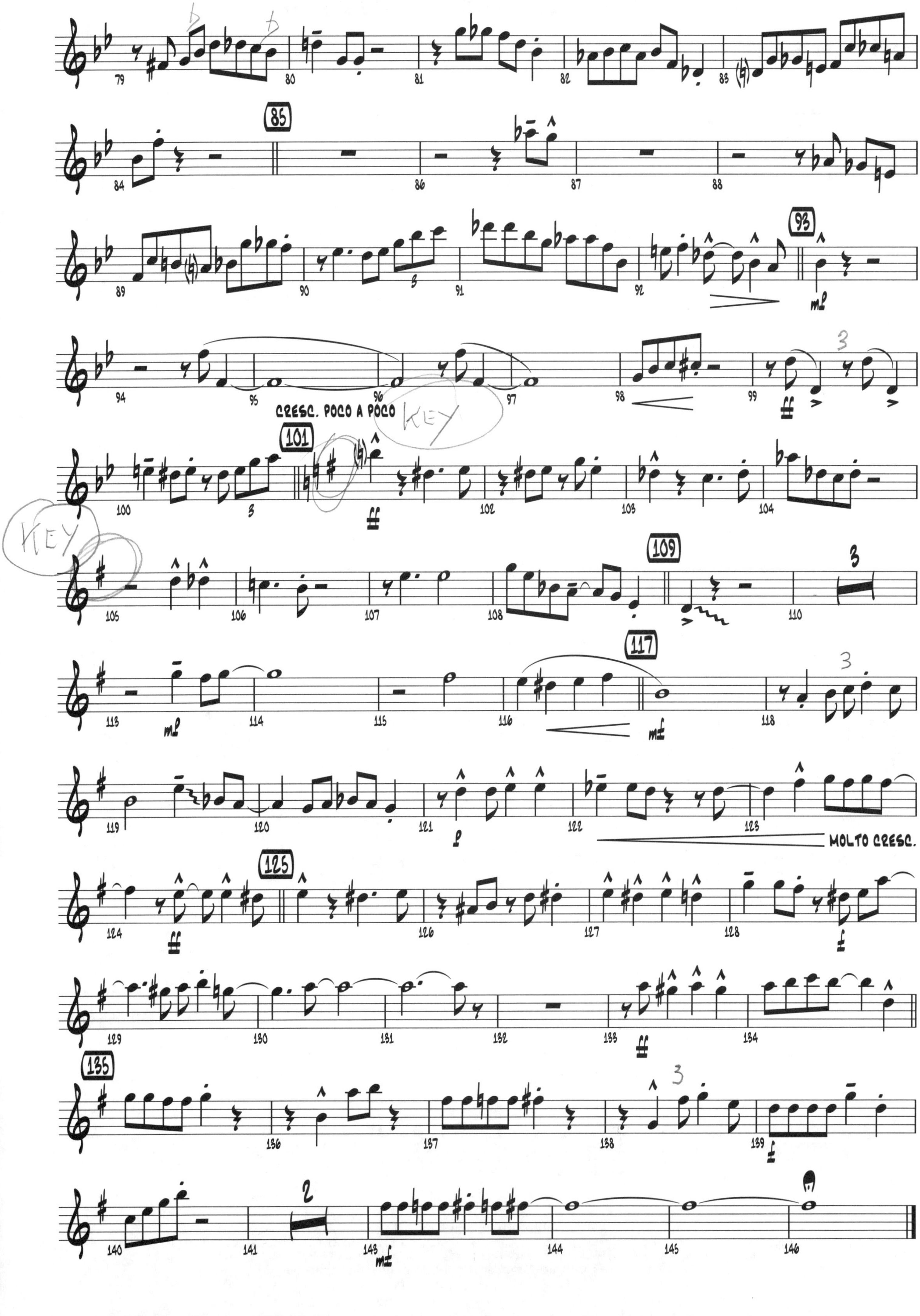
85
93
mf
CRESC. POCO A POCO
ff
101
KEY
109
117
mf
MOLTO CRESC.
125
135

MY FOOLISH HEART

1st E♭ Alto Saxophone

Words by NED WASHINGTON
Music by VICTOR YOUNG
Arranged by DAVE RIVELLO

COUNT 4 X 8 BARS.
8 BARS.
38
2 SOLO (OPT. AD LIB.)
AMI7/G
F#13 SUS
F#13(b9)
BMI9
EMI9
Bb13
AMI9
AMI7(b5)
D7(b9)
46
GMAJ9
8 BARS.
DMI9
G9
CMAJ9
F#MI7(b5)
EMI9
A13
AMI11
D13
54
PIANO OR GUITAR
BRASS STAND
ALTO'S
62
70
ME
SOLO
78
NOT ME
SOLO
SLOW.
FREELY (OPT. AD LIB.)
CMAJ7

GET IT ON

1st E♭ Alto Saxophone

Words and Music by BILL CHASE
and TERRY RICHARDS
Arranged by VICTOR LOPEZ

© 1969 (Renewed) CHA BIL MUSIC
This Arrangement © 2007 CHA BIL MUSIC
All Rights Reserved including Public Performance   Used by Permission

To Coda
mf
cresc.
43
ff
Repeat 3 times
Open for Solos (Tbn., Tpt. & T. Sax)
background figures on cue behind Solos
51
ff
fp
fp
fp
1-2.
mf
3.
mf
cresc.
D.S. 𝄋 al Coda
Coda
ff
69
a tempo

THIS CAN'T BE LOVE

From "The Boys From Syracuse"

1st E♭ Alto Saxophone

Words by LORENZ HART
Music by RICHARD RODGERS
Arranged by LISA DeSPAIN

Medium swing ♩ = ca. 120

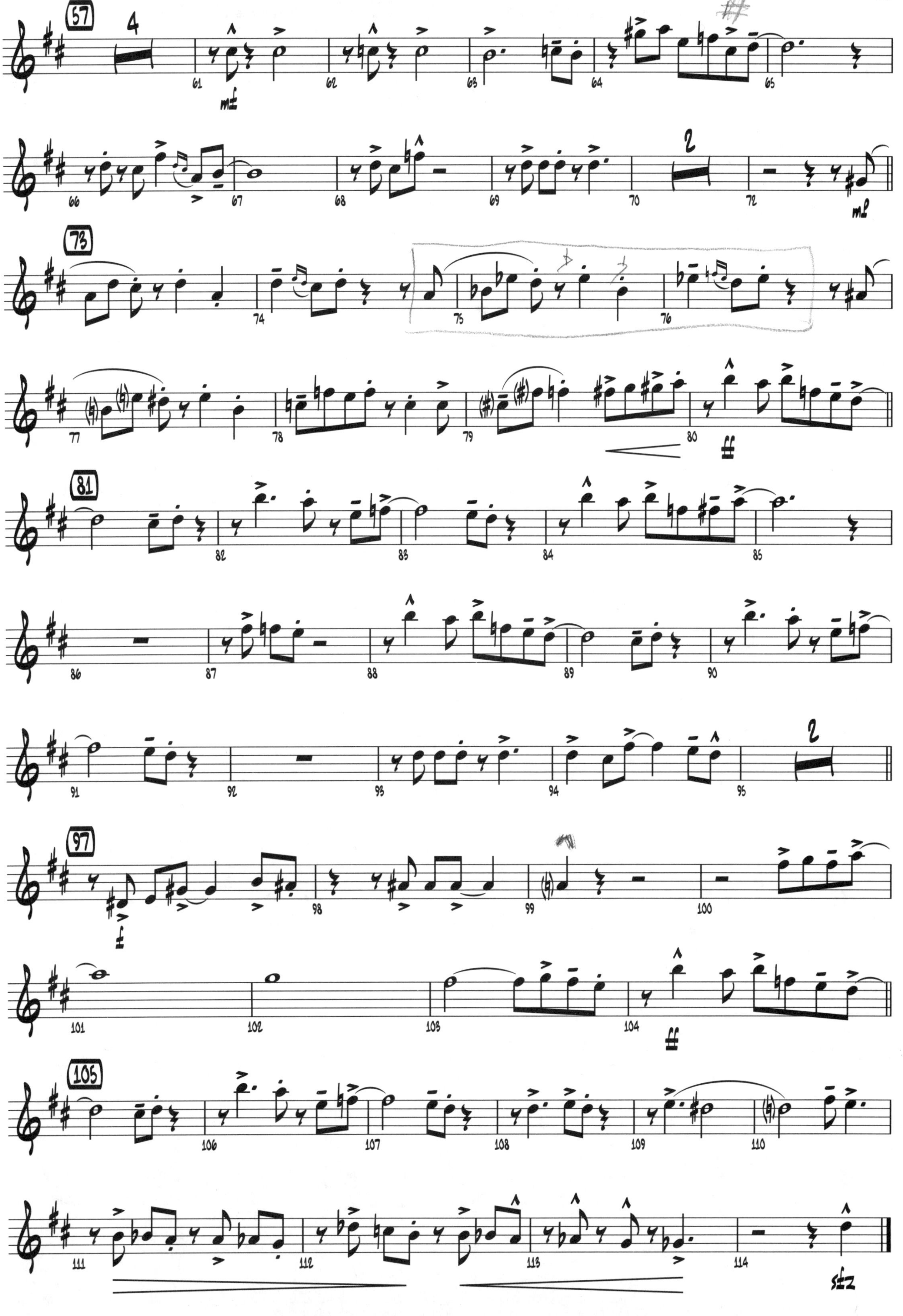57
mf
73
81
ff
97
f
105
sfz

OH, LADY BE GOOD!

1ST E♭ ALTO SAXOPHONE

Music and Lyrics by
GEORGE GERSHWIN and IRA GERSHWIN
Arranged by TERRY WHITE

33
41
49
57
SOLO
GMAJ7
EM7
A7(#5)
DMAJ7
BM
BM(MAJ7)
BM7
E9
EM7
A7
A7(b9)
65
DMAJ7
G13
DMAJ7
D#°7
EM7
A7(b9)
DMAJ7
EM7
A7(b9)
73
END SOLO

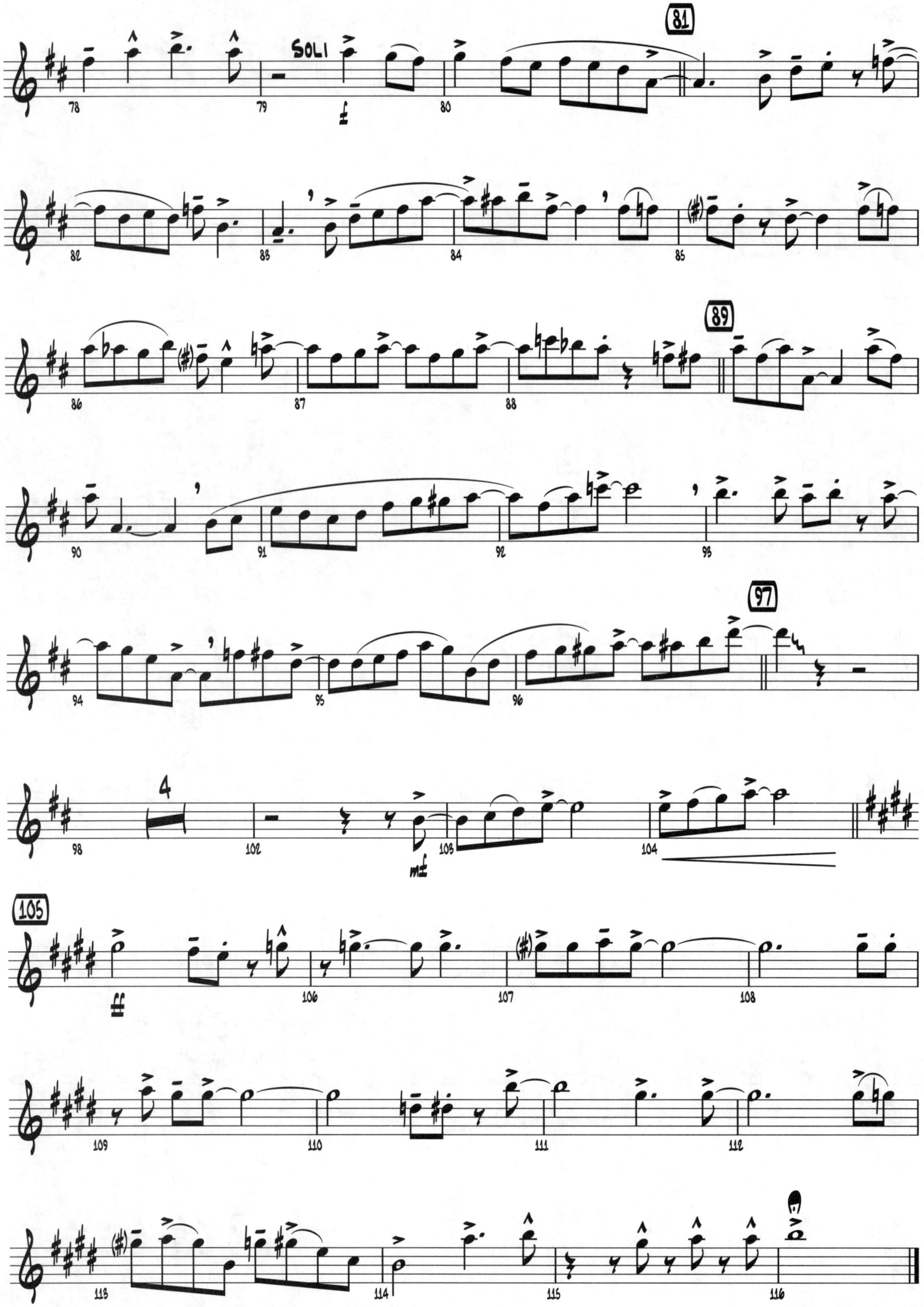
81
SOLI
89
97
4
105

This page left blank intentionally to facilitate page turns.

JUMPIN' AT THE WOODSIDE

1st Eb Alto Saxophone

By COUNT BASIE
Arranged by RICH DeROSA

75
83
91
99
107
115
123
131
139
147
mf
REPEAT
2 TIMES
SOLO
PLAY LAST TIME
NOT EARLY
99 - 130

155
mf
163 OPTIONAL ENCORE TAG #1 (FROM PICK-UPS TO 163 - WITH REPEATS - TO FINE)
2ND TIME ONLY
2nd TIME NO GAP
1.
2.
TACET ON OPTIONALTAG #2
mf
173 OPTIONAL ENCORE TAG #2 (FROM PICK-UPS TO 173 TO FINE)
f
BE NEAT
FINE
OPTIONAL ENCORE TAG #3

This page left blank intentionally to facilitate page turns.

SUMMERTIME

By GEORGE GERSHWIN,
DuBOSE and DOROTHY HEYWARD
and IRA GERSHWIN
Arranged by DAVE RIVELLO

1st E♭ Alto Saxophone

Tempo ♩ = 110 - 120 Swing feel

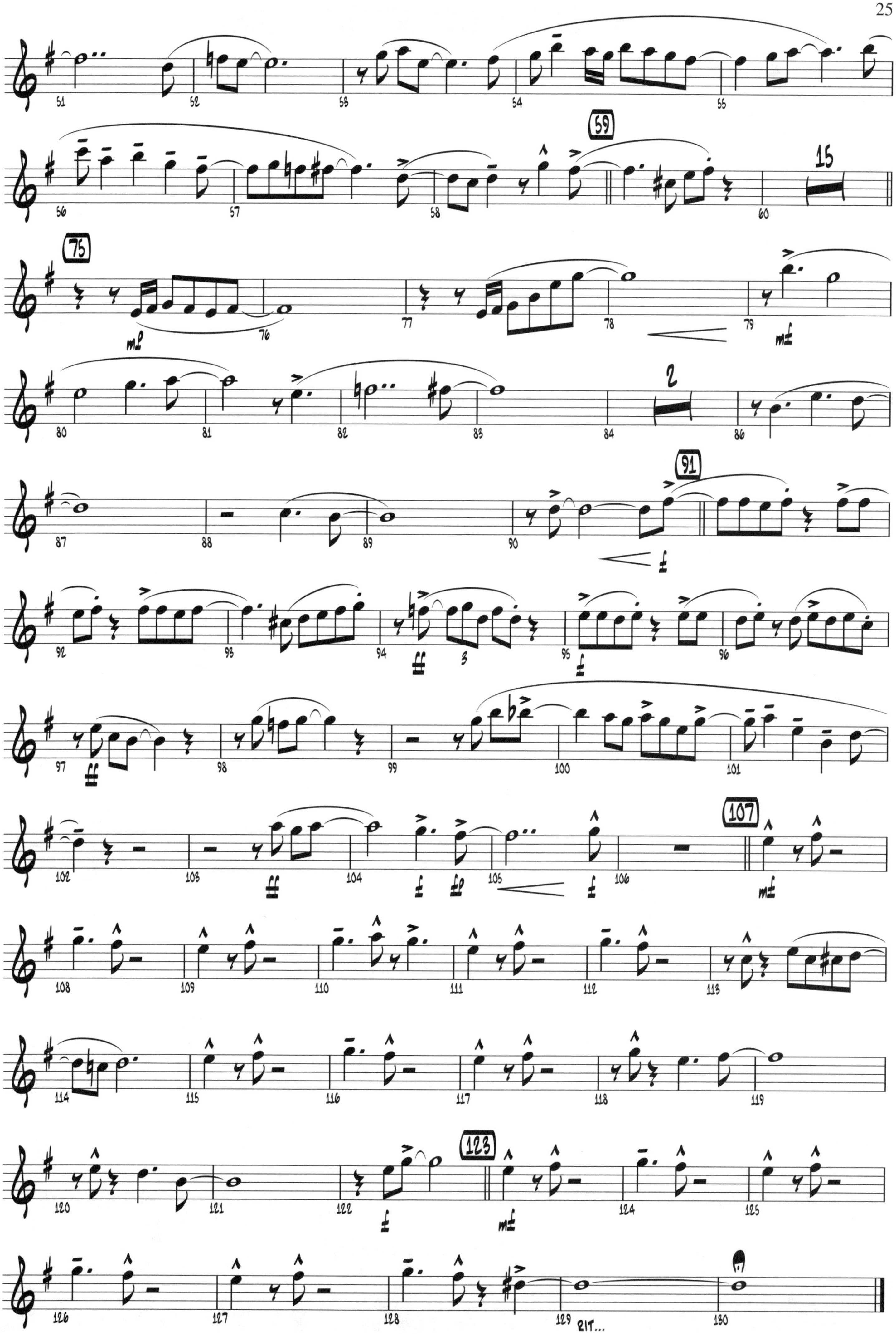
59
15
75
mf
mf
2
91
f
ff
3
f
ff
ff
f
fp
f
107
mf
123
f
mf
RIT...

GREENSLEEVES

1st E♭ Alto Saxophone

Traditional
Arranged by GREG YASINITSKY

© 2006 Alfred Music Publishing Co., Inc.
All Rights Reserved

REPEAT
NO BACKINGS
PAUL LAST
NO BACKINGS
NO BACKINGS
NO BACKINGS

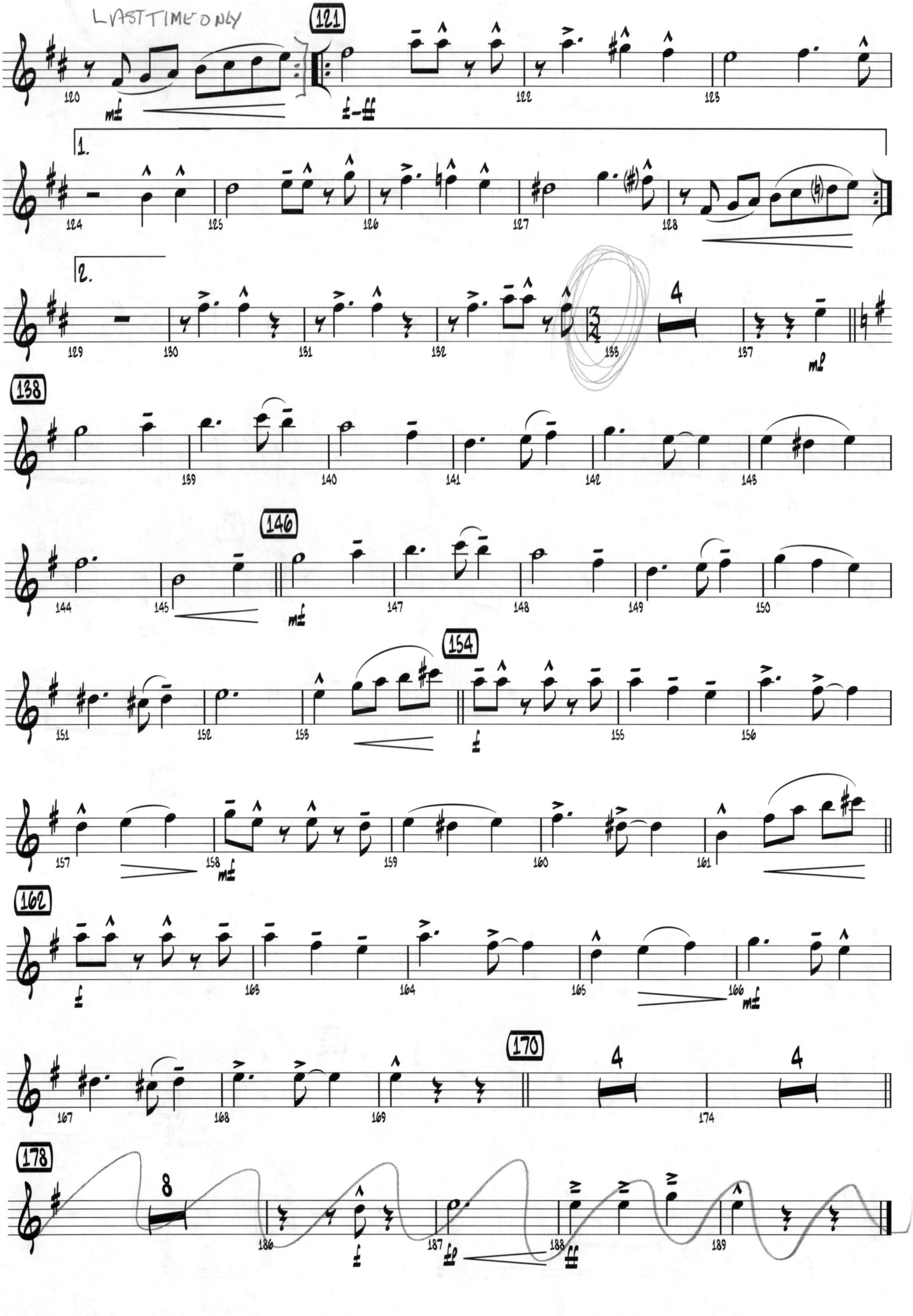
LAST TIME ONLY
121
1.
2.
138
146
154
162
170
178
mf
f–ff
f
fp
ff